PRAYER IS THE ANSWER

Classic Writings on Prayer

E. M. BOUNDS,
ANDREW MURRAY,
AND JOHN WESLEY

SMITH FREEMAN Publishing

Prayer Is the Answer Classic Writings On Prayer

ISBN: 978-0-9997706-3-4

Bible Passages

All Bible passages in this text are taken from the following translations:

KJV: The Holy Bible, King James Version

NKJV: Scripture taken from the New King James Version.

Editor's Note

All original texts included in this book are derived from various books, tracts, and sermons, all of which are in the public domain. The essays in this text have been edited and abridged for modern readers. In all cases, the editors have endeavored to preserve the authors' original intent.

Cover design by Kim Russell | Wahoo Designs

Table of Contents

About the Authors

John Wesley (1703–1791) was an English clergyman, a theologian, and one of the founders of Methodism. Wesley wrote or edited over 400 publications including several books which remain Methodist doctrinal standards. Over 300 years after his death, Wesley continues to be an important theological influence on Methodists and Methodist-heritage groups. Generations of Christians have been influenced and uplifted by his writings, his teachings, his sermons, and his example.

Andrew Murray (1828-1917) was a South African pastor and teacher who wrote over fifty books, many of which he authored in both Dutch and English. In a letter to his parents, Murray once wrote, "Your son has been born again. I have cast myself on Christ." He did, indeed, cast himself with Christ during sixty years of ministry in the Dutch Reformed Church of South Africa. He wrote extensively on Christian spirituality and the power of prayer.

Edward McKendree Bounds (1835-1913) was an American Methodist minister who wrote eleven books, nine of which were on the topic of prayer. At the age of twenty-four, Bounds was called to become the pastor of a small congregation in Monticello, Missouri. Thus began a lifelong ministry that lasted over fifty years. Bounds, who regularly began his day with several hours of predawn meditation and prayer, was profoundly influenced by the works of John Wesley.

INTRODUCTION

The effective, fervent prayer
of a righteous man avails much.

JAMES 5:16 NKJV

Each new day provides countless opportunities to put God where He belongs: at the center of our lives. When we do, we worship Him, not only with our words and deeds, but also with our prayers. And, as E. M. Bounds correctly observed, "To pray is the greatest thing we can do . . . true praying has the largest results for good . . . we cannot do too much of real praying."

Twenty-first-century life can be complicated and stressful. Yet, whatever problems we may encounter, whatever questions we may have, prayer is the answer. No problems are too big for our Creator, and no circumstances are too is significant to escape His gaze. When we petition Him in prayer, He changes our world and—just as importantly—He changes us.

The writings in this text reveal the thoughts,

the reflections, the guidance, and the observations of three well-known Christian pastors: John Wesley, Andrew Murray, and E. M. Bounds. All three men wrote prolifically on the subject of prayer, and the ideas contained on these pages reflect their belief that prayer is the answer to the world's problems, as well as our own.

When we weave the habit of prayer into the very fabric of our days, we invite God to become a partner in every aspect of our lives. When we consult Him on an hourly basis, we avail ourselves of His wisdom, His strength, and His love. So today, instead of turning things over in your mind, turn them over to the Lord in prayer. Instead of worrying about your next decision, let your heavenly Father lead the way. Don't limit your prayers to mealtime or bedtime. Pray constantly about things great and small. God is listening, and He wants to hear from you. Now.

God rules the world by the prayers of His saints.
Prayer is the power by which Satan is conquered.
It is by prayer that the church on earth has
at its disposal the powers of the heavenly world.

ANDREW MURRAY

1

Lord, Teach Us to Pray

By Andrew Murray

Now it came to pass, as He was praying in a certain place, when He ceased, that one of His disciples said to Him, "Lord, teach us to pray, as John also taught his disciples."

LUKE 11:1 NKJV

The disciples had been with Christ, and they had seen Him pray. They had learned to understand something of the connection between His wondrous life in public and His secret life of prayer. They had learned to believe in Him as a Master in the art of prayer—none could pray like Him. And so they came to Him with this request: "Lord, teach us to pray." And in later years, they would have told us that there were few teachings more wonderful or blessed than His lessons on prayer.

As we grow in the Christian life, the thought and the faith of the Beloved Master in His never-failing intercession becomes more precious, and the hope of being like Christ in His intercession gains an attractiveness before unknown. And as we see Him pray—and remember that there is none who can pray like Him, and none who can teach like Him—we feel that the petition of the disciples, "Lord, teach us to pray," is just what we need. As we think about Him—how He Himself is our very own, how He is Himself our life—we feel assured that we have but to ask, and He will be delighted to take us up into a closer fellowship with Himself, and He will teach us to pray even as He prays.

Come, my brothers! Shall we not go to the Blessed Master and ask Him to enroll our names anew in that school which He always keeps open for those who long to continue their studies in the Divine art of prayer and intercession? Yes, let us this very day say to the Master, as they did of old, "Lord, teach us to pray." As we meditate, we shall find each word of that request to be full of meaning.

"Lord, teach us to pray." Yes, to pray. This is what we need to be taught. Though in its beginnings prayer is so simple that the child can pray, yet it is at the same time the highest and holiest work to which man can rise. It is fellowship with the Unseen and Most Holy One. The powers of the eternal world have been placed at its disposal. It is the very essence of true religion, the channel of all blessings, the secret of power and life. It is through prayer that God has given us the right to take hold of Him and His strength, not only for ourselves, but also for others, for the Church, and for the world.

It is on prayer that the promises wait for their fulfilment, the kingdom waits for its coming, and the glory of God waits for its full revelation. And for this blessed work, how sluggish and unfit we are. It is only the Spirit of God who can enable us to do it aright. How speedily we are deceived into a resting in the form, while the power is wanting. Our early training, the teaching of the Church, the influence of habit, the stirring of the emotions —how easily these lead to prayer which has no spiritual power, and avails little. True prayer—the kind that takes hold of God's strength, that avails much, to which the gates of heaven are really opened wide—this is what we seek. And this is what we need.

From *Lord, Teach Us to Pray*

2

People of Prayer Needed

By E. M. Bounds

*Go therefore and make disciples of all the nations,
baptizing them in the name of the Father
and of the Son and of the Holy Spirit, teaching them
to observe all things that I have commanded you;
and lo, I am with you always, even to the end of the age.*

MATTHEW 28:19-20 NKJV

We are constantly on a stretch, if not on a strain, to devise new methods, new plans, new organizations to advance the Church and enlarge the gospel. This trend has a tendency to lose sight of the person—or even to sink the person—who is in the plan or inside the organization. God's plan is to make much of the man, far more of him than of anything else. People are God's method. The Church is looking for better methods; God is looking for better people.

"There was a man sent from God, whose name was John" (John 1:6). The dispensation that heralded and prepared the way for Christ was bound up in that man John. "Unto us a child is born, unto us a son is given" (Isaiah 9:6 KJV). The world's salvation comes out of that cradled Son.

When Paul appeals to the personal character of the people who rooted the gospel in the world, he solves the mystery of their success. The glory and efficiency of the gospel is staked on the people who proclaim it.

When God declares that "the eyes of the LORD run to and fro throughout the whole earth, to show himself strong in the behalf of them whose heart is perfect toward him" (2 Chronicles 16:9 KJV), He declares the necessity of people and His dependence on them as a channel through which to exert His power upon the world. This vital truth is one that this age of machinery is apt to forget. The forgetting of it is as baneful on the work of God as would be the striking of the sun from His sphere. Darkness, confusion, and death would ensue.

What the Church needs today is not more or better machinery, not new organizations or novel methods. The Church needs people whom the Holy Spirit can use—people of prayer, people mighty in prayer.

From *Power Through Prayer*

3

The Golden Rule and Prayer

By John Wesley

Therefore all things whatsoever ye would that men should do to you, do ye even so to them: for this is the law and the prophets.

MATTHEW 7:12 KJV

So that your prayer may have its full weight with God, see that you have charity toward all men. Otherwise your prayer is more likely to bring a curse than a blessing on your own head. Nor can you expect to receive any blessing from God while you have not charity towards your neighbor. Therefore, let this hindrance be removed without delay. Confirm your love towards one another, and love them, not in word only, but also in deed and in truth.

"Therefore all things whatsoever ye would that men should do to you, do ye even so to them; for this is the law and the prophets." This is that royal law, that golden rule of mercy as well as justice, which even the heathen Emperor caused to be written over the gate of his palace. It is a rule which many believe to be naturally engraved on the mind of everyone who comes into the world. And this much is certain: It is a law that it commends itself, as soon as it is heard, to every man's conscience and understanding. Therefore no man can knowingly offend against this royal law without carrying his condemnation in his own breast.

Never do unto another person what you would not want that he should do unto you. When you follow this rule, you will never again judge your neighbor; you will never causelessly or lightly think evil of anyone, nor will you speak evil. And, you will never mention even the real fault of an absent person unless you are convinced it is absolutely needful for the good of other souls.

From *Upon Our Lord's Sermon on the Mount*

4

None Can Teach Like Jesus

By Andrew Murray

And Jesus, when He came out, saw a great multitude
and was moved with compassion for them,
because they were like sheep not having a shepherd.
So He began to teach them many things.

MARK 6:34 NKJV

Jesus has opened a school in which He trains His redeemed ones, the ones who specially desire it, to have power in prayer. Let us enter it with this petition, "Lord! It is just this we need to be taught: O teach us, Lord, to pray."

Dear Lord, we have read in Your Word with

what power Your believing people of old used to pray, and we have read about the mighty wonders that were done in answer to their prayers. And if this took place under the Old Covenant, in the time of preparation, how much more will You, in these days of fulfilment, give Your people this sure sign of Your presence in their midst?

We have heard the promises given to Your apostles concerning the power of prayer, and we have seen how gloriously they experienced their truth. We hear continually about the glorious tokens of Your power that You still give to those who trust You fully. Lord, we are like the men of old, so teach us to pray like them. Your promises are for us, too, as are the powers and gifts of the heavenly world. So teach us to pray so that we may receive abundantly.

Yes, we feel the need now of being taught to pray. At first there is no work that appears so simple; later on, none that is more difficult. So the confession is forced from us: We do not know how to pray as we should. It is true we have God's Word, with its clear and sure promises, but sin has so darkened our minds that we do not always know how to apply the Word.

In spiritual things we do not always seek the most needful things. In temporal things we are do not always avail ourselves of the wonderful liberty our Father has given us: the liberty to ask for what we need. And even when we know what to ask for, much is still needed to make prayer acceptable. Our prayers must be to the glory of God, in full surrender to His will, in full assurance of faith, in the name of Jesus, and with a perseverance that, if need be, refuses to be denied. All this must be learned. It can only be learned in the school of much prayer, because practice makes perfect. Amid the painful consciousness of ignorance and unworthiness, in the struggle between believing and doubting, the heavenly art of effectual prayer is learned. And none can teach like Jesus.

A pupil needs a teacher who knows his work, who has the gift of teaching, who in patience and love will descend to the pupil's needs. Jesus is all this and much more. It is Jesus, praying Himself, who teaches us to pray. He knows what prayer is. He learned it amid the trials and tears of His earthly life. In heaven it is still His beloved work: His life there is prayer.

Nothing delights Jesus more than to find those whom He can take with Him into the Father's presence, whom He can clothe with the power to pray down God's blessing on those around them, whom He can train to be His fellow workers in the intercession by which the kingdom is to be revealed on earth. He knows how to teach. By His Holy Spirit, He has access to our hearts, and teaches us to pray by showing us the sin that hinders the prayer, or giving us the assurance that we please God. He teaches, by giving not only thoughts of *what* to ask—or *how* to ask—but also by breathing within us the very spirit of prayer, by living within us as the Great Intercessor.

Jesus never taught His disciples how to preach, only how to pray. He did not speak much of preaching well, but He spoke much of praying well. Knowing how to speak to God is more important than knowing how to speak to man. Not power with men, but power with God, is the first thing. Jesus loves to teach us how to pray.

From *Lord, Teach Us to Pray*

5

MUCH TIME SHOULD BE GIVEN TO PRAYER

By E. M. Bounds

So He Himself often withdrew into the wilderness and prayed.

LUKE 5:16 NKJV

Many private prayers must be short, and public prayers, as a rule, should be short and condensed. But in our private communions with God, time is a feature essential to its value. Much time spent with God is the secret of all successful praying.

Prayer which is felt as a mighty force is the product of much time spent with the Lord. Our short prayers owe their point and efficiency to the long ones that have preceded them. The short prevailing prayer cannot be prayed by one who has not prevailed with God in a mightier struggle of long continuance.

Jacob's victory of faith could not have been gained without that all-night wrestling. God's acquaintance is not made by pop calls. God does not bestow His gifts on the casual or hasty comers and goers. Much time spent with God alone is the secret of knowing Him and of influence with Him. He yields to the persistency of a faith that knows Him. He bestows His richest gifts upon those who declare their desire for, and appreciation of, those gifts by the constancy as well as earnestness of their prayers.

Christ, who in this as well as other things is our Example, spent many whole nights in prayer. His custom was to pray much. He had His habitual place to pray. Many long seasons of praying make up His history and character.

Paul prayed day and night. It took time away from very important interests for Daniel to pray three times a day. And, David's morning, noon, and nighttime prayers were doubtless, on many occasions, protracted. While we have no specific account of the time these Bible saints spent in prayer, we have indications that they consumed much time in prayer. And, on some occasions long seasons of praying was their custom. While the value of their prayers cannot be measured by the clock, we must still understand the value—and the necessity—of being much alone with God. If this feature has not been produced by our faith, then our faith is weak and superficial.

The men who have most fully illustrated Christ in their characters, and have most powerfully affected the world for Him, have been men who spent so much time with God as to make it a notable feature of their lives.

From *Power Through Prayer*

6

Ask and It Shall Be Given

By Andrew Murray

So I say to you, ask, and it will be given to you; seek, and you will find; knock, and it will be opened to you. For everyone who asks receives, and he who seeks finds, and to him who knocks it will be opened.

LUKE 11:9–10 NKJV

God's giving is inseparably connected with our asking. He applies this especially to the Holy Spirit. As surely as a father on earth gives bread to His child, so God gives the Holy Spirit to them that ask Him. The whole ministration of the Spirit is ruled by the one great law: God must give; we must ask.

When the Holy Spirit was poured out at Pentecost with a flow that never ceases, it was in answer to prayer. The inflow into a believer's heart, and His outflow in the rivers of living water still depend upon the law: "Ask, and it shall be given." Perhaps nowhere do we see this more clearly than in the first half of the Acts of the Apostles. The story of the birth of the Church in the outpouring of the Holy Spirit will teach us how to pray.

We begin with the familiar words of Acts 1:14: "These all continued with one accord in prayer and supplication." And then there follows: "And when the day of Pentecost was fully come, they were all with one accord in one place" (Acts 2:1 KJV). "And they were all filled with the Holy Ghost" (Acts 2:4). "And the same day there were added unto them about three thousand souls" (Acts 2:41). The great work of redemption had been accomplished. The Holy Spirit had been promised by Christ "not many days hence." He had sat down on His throne and received the Spirit from the Father. But all this was not enough. One thing more was needed: the ten days' united continued supplication of the disciples. It was intense, continued prayer that prepared the disciples' hearts, intense prayer that opened the windows of heaven, and intense prayer that brought down the promised gift.

For all the ages the law is laid down here: At the birth of the Church, that whatever else may be found on earth, the power of the Spirit must be prayed down from heaven. Continued prayer will be the measure of the Spirit's working in the Church. Direct, definite, determined prayer is what we need.

Peter and John had been brought before the Council and threatened with punishment. When they returned to their brethren and reported what had been said to them; "all lifted up their voice to God with one accord," and prayed for boldness to speak the word. "And when they had prayed, the place was shaken . . . ; and they were all filled with the Holy Ghost, and they spake the word of God with boldness. And the multitude of them that believed were of one heart and of one soul. . . . And with great power gave the apostles witness of the resurrection of the Lord Jesus: and great grace was upon them all" (Acts 4).

It is as if the story of Pentecost is repeated a second time over— with the prayer, the shaking of the house, the filling with the Spirit, the speaking

God's word with boldness and power, the great grace upon all, the manifestation of unity and love — to imprint it on the heart of the Church. It is prayer that lies at the root of the spiritual life and power of the Church. The measure of God's giving the Spirit is our asking.

He gives as a father to him who asks as a child.

From *The Ministry of Intercession: A Plea for More Prayer*

7

Pray Without Ceasing and Walk in the Ways of God

By John Wesley

Rejoice always, pray without ceasing,
in everything give thanks;
for this is the will of God in Christ Jesus for you.
1 THESSALONIANS 5:16–18 NKJV

Strive to pray without ceasing; at all times, in all places, lifting up your heart to God until you "awake up after his likeness" and are "satisfied with it."

"Strive to enter in at the strait gate" (Luke 13:24 KJV), not only by this agony of soul, of conviction, of sorrow, of shame, of desire, of fear, of unceasing prayer; but likewise by ordering your conversations in righteousness, by walking with all your strength in all the ways of God, in the ways of innocence, of piety, and of mercy.

Abstain from all appearance of evil.

Do all possible good to all men.

Deny yourself and your own will.

In all things, take up your cross daily.

Be ready to cut off your right hand, to pluck out your right eye and to cast it away. Be willing to suffer the loss of possessions, friends, health, and all things on earth, so you may enter into the kingdom of heaven!

Do you walk in all the ordinances of God? In public, with family, in private prayer? If not, if you habitually neglect any one of these known duties, how can you expect that the light of His countenance should continue to shine upon you? Make haste to "strengthen the things that remain;" then your soul shall live.

From *Upon Our Lord's Sermon on the Mount*
and from *The Wilderness State*

8

Pray and Worship in Spirit and in Truth

By Andrew Murray

But the hour cometh, and now is, when the true worshippers shall worship the Father in spirit and in truth: for the Father seeketh such to worship him. God is a Spirit: and they that worship him must worship him in spirit and in truth.

JOHN 4:23–24 KJV

These words of Jesus to the woman of Samaria are His first recorded teaching on the subject of prayer. These words give us some wonderful first glimpses into the world of prayer. The Father seeks worshippers. Our worship satisfies His loving heart and is a joy to Him. He seeks true worshippers, but finds many who fall short.

True worship is that which is in spirit and truth. The Son has come to open the way for genuine worship, and He has come in order to teach it to us. So one of our first lessons in the school of prayer must be to understand what it means to pray in spirit and in truth, and how we can attain it.

To the woman of Samaria our Lord spoke of three types of worship. There is, first, the ignorant worship of the Samaritans: "Ye worship ye know not what." The second is the intelligent worship of the Jew, having the true knowledge of God: "We know what we worship: for salvation is of the Jews." Then, the Lord described the new, spiritual worship which He Himself had come to introduce: "The hour is coming, and is now, when the true worshippers shall worship the Father in spirit and truth" (John 4:22–23).

In examining these three types of worship, it is evident that the words "in spirit and truth" do not mean, as is often thought, "from the heart, with sincerity." The Samaritans had the five books of Moses and some knowledge of God; there was doubtless more than one among them who honestly and earnestly sought God in prayer. The Jews had the true full revelation of God in His word, as had thus far been given; there were among them godly men who called upon God with their whole heart. And yet these godly men had not worshipped "in spirit and truth" in the full meaning of those words. Jesus said, "The hour is coming, and now is." So it is only *in* Him and *through* Him that the worship of God will be in spirit and truth.

Among Christians one still finds these three classes of worshippers. We find some worshippers who, in their ignorance, hardly know what they ask. They pray earnestly, yet receive little. We see other worshippers who have more correct knowledge, who try to pray with all their minds and hearts. They often pray most earnestly, and yet do not attain to the full blessedness of worship in spirit and truth. So, we must strive to place ourselves in the third class, and we must ask our Lord Jesus to take us there. We must be taught by Him how to worship in spirit and truth. This alone is spiritual worship; this makes us worshippers such as the Father seeks. In prayer everything will depend on our understanding well—and practicing—the worship in spirit and in truth.

There must be harmony between God and His worshippers; such as God is, so must His worship be. The man who would truly worship God, who would find and know and possess and enjoy God, must be in harmony with Him, and must have a capacity for receiving Him. Because God is Spirit, we must worship in spirit. As God is, so must His worshipper be.

And what does this mean? The woman had asked our Lord whether Samaria or Jerusalem was the true place of worship. He answers that henceforth worship is no longer to be limited to a certain place: "Woman, believe Me, the hour cometh when ye shall neither in this mountain, nor yet at Jerusalem, worship the Father" (John 4:21). As God is Spirit, not bound by space or time, but in His infinite perfection always and everywhere the same, so His worship would henceforth no longer be confined by place or form. This is a lesson of deep importance. God is a spirit: He is the Everlasting and Unchangeable One. What He is, He is always and in truth. So our worship must be in spirit and truth.

From *Lord, Teach Us to Pray*

9

Set Regular Times for Prayer and Continue Praying Throughout the Day

By Andrew Murray

So He Himself often withdrew into the wilderness and prayed.

LUKE 5:16 NKJV

Pray without ceasing. Does this refer to continual acts of prayer in which we are to persevere? Or does it refer to the spirit of prayerfulness that should animate us all throughout the day? It includes both. The example of our Lord Jesus shows us this. We are to enter our closet for special seasons of prayer; we are at times to persevere there in persistent prayer. We are also to walk in God's presence throughout the day, with the whole heart set upon heavenly things. Without set times of prayer, the spirit of prayer will be dull and weak. Without the continual prayerfulness, the set times will not avail.

Are we to pray for ourselves or others? The answer, of course, is both. Too many people care—and pray—only about themselves. This is a profound mistake. It is only when the branch gives itself to bear fruit, more fruit, much fruit, that it can live a healthy life and expect a rich inflow of sap. The death of Christ brought Him to the place of everlasting intercession. Your death with Him to sin and self sets you free from the care of self, which elevates you to the dignity of intercessor—one who can get life and blessing from God for others.

Know your calling. Begin this your work. Give yourself wholly to it. Pray in the closet and pray throughout the day. This is the example our Lord Jesus has shown us.

From *The Ministry of Intercession: A Plea for More Prayer*

10

Let Us Ask for His Blessings

By John Wesley

Ask, and it will be given to you; seek, and you will find; knock, and it will be opened to you. For everyone who asks receives, and he who seeks finds, and to him who knocks it will be opened.

MATTHEW 7:7–8 NKJV

If He is a Father, then He is good, and He is loving to His children. And here is the first and great reason for prayer. God is willing to bless; let us ask for a blessing. He raised us from the dust of the earth; He breathed into us the breath of life, and we became living souls. Let us ask of Him, and He will not withhold any good thing from the work of His own hands.

He is our Preserver; who, day by day, sustains the life He has given. From His continuing love we receive life, and breath, and all things. So let us boldly come to Him, and we shall "obtain mercy and find grace to help in time of need" (Hebrews 4:16).

Above all, He is the Father of our Lord Jesus Christ, and of all that believe in Him. It is He who justifies us "freely by his grace, through the redemption that is in Jesus" (Romans 3:24). It is He who has "blotted out all our sins, and healed all our infirmities." It is He who has received us as His own children, by adoption and grace. It is He who "has begotten us again of incorruptible seed", and "created us anew in Christ Jesus." Therefore we know that He hears us always. So we pray to Him without ceasing. We pray because we love; and "we love Him because He first loved us" (1 John 4:19).

From *Upon Our Lord's Sermon on the Mount*

11

A Secret Place to Pray

By Andrew Murray

And in the morning, rising up a great while before day, he went out, and departed into a solitary place, and there prayed.

MARK 1:35 KJV

After Jesus had called His first disciples, He gave them their first public teaching when He delivered the Sermon on the Mount. It was there that He expounded on the kingdom of God, its laws, and its life. In that kingdom, God is not only King, but also Father; He not only gives all, but is Himself all. In the knowledge and fellowship of Him alone is its blessedness.

Hence it came, as a matter of course, that the revelation of prayer and the prayer life was a part of Christ's teaching concerning the New Kingdom He came to set up. Moses gave neither command nor regulation with regard to prayer. Even the prophets say little directly concerning the duty of prayer; it is Jesus who teaches us how to pray. And the first thing the Lord teaches His disciples is that they must have a secret place for prayer.

Everyone must have some solitary spot where he can be alone with his God. Every teacher must have a schoolroom. We have learned to know and accept Jesus as our only teacher in the school of prayer. He has already taught us at Samaria that worship is no longer confined to times and places; that worship, spiritual true worship, is a thing of the spirit and the life. The whole man must, in his whole life, worship in spirit and truth. And yet Jesus wants each one to choose for himself the fixed spot where he can daily meet Him.

That inner chamber, that solitary place, is Jesus' schoolroom. That spot may be anywhere; that spot may change from day to day if we change our abode; but a secret place there must be. It is there, in quiet, that the pupil places himself in the Master's presence, to be prepared by Him to worship the Father. There alone, but there most surely, Jesus comes to us and teaches us to pray.

From *Lord, Teach Us to Pray*

12

The Power of Prayer

By Andrew Murray

The effective, fervent prayer
of a righteous man avails much.
JAMES 5:16 NKJV

Prayer is the one power on earth that commands the power of heaven. The story of the early days of the Church is God's great object lesson, to teach His Church what prayer can do, how it alone, but it most surely, can draw down the treasures and powers of heaven into the life of earth.

Prayer is at once indispensable and irresistible. Do we not see how unknown and untold power and blessing is stored up for us in heaven? Can we not understand how that power will make us a blessing to men, and fit us to do any work or face any danger? Do we not trust the promise that those who have the heavenly power can pray it down upon others?

How, in all the discussions between ministers and people—in all the ministrations of Christ's Church—is prayer the one secret of success? How can it defy all the power of the world and fit men to conquer that world for Christ? The answer, of course, is that the power of the heavenly life, the power of God's own Spirit, the power of Omnipotence, waits for prayer to bring it down.

In this type of prayer, there was little thought of personal need or happiness. If we wish be delivered from the sin of restraining prayer, we must enlarge our hearts for the work of intercession. The attempt to pray constantly for ourselves must be a failure. It is in intercession for others that our faith and love and perseverance will be aroused, and that power of the Spirit will be found. This power can fit us for saving men.

When we ask how we can become more faithful and successful in prayer, we must see how the Master teaches us in the parable of the Friend at Midnight:

> And He said to them, "Which of you shall have a friend, and go to him at midnight and say to him, 'Friend, lend me three loaves; for a friend of mine has come to me on his journey, and I have nothing to set before him'; and he will answer from within and say, 'Do not trouble me; the door is now shut, and my children are with me in bed; I cannot rise and give to you'? I say to you, though he will not rise and give to him because he is his friend, yet because of his persistence he will rise and give him as many as he needs. So I say to you, ask, and it will be given to you; seek, and you will find; knock, and it will be opened to you. For everyone who asks receives, and he who seeks finds, and to him who knocks it will be opened." *Luke 11:5–10 NKJV*

Intercession for others is the most perfect form of prayer: it is the prayer Christ prays on His throne. Let us learn what the elements of true intercession are.

In our intercession we may find that there is difficulty and delay with the answer. It may be as if God says, "I cannot give to thee." In such circumstances, it is not easy, against all appearances, to hold fast to our confidence that He will hear us. It is not easy to persevere in full assurance that we shall eventually have what we ask. Yet this type of perseverance and trust is what God looks for from us. He so highly prizes our confidence in Him—it is essentially the highest honor that the creature can render the Creator—that He will do anything to train us in the exercise of trusting Him.

Blessed is the man who is not staggered by God's delay or silence or apparent refusal; blessed is he who is strong in faith, giving glory to God. Such faith perseveres, if need be, and cannot fail to inherit the blessing.

In the parable above, note the certainty of a rich reward. Oh that we might learn to believe in the certainty of an abundant answer. If we will but believe in God and His faithfulness, intercession will become the very first thing we take refuge in when we seek blessing for others, and the very last thing for which we cannot find time. Intercession will become a thing of joy and hope because we know that we are sowing seed that will bring forth fruit a hundredfold. Disappointment is impossible.

Let all lovers of souls, and all workers in the service of the gospel, take courage. Time spent in prayer will yield more than that given to work. Prayer alone gives work its worth and its success.

Prayer opens the way for God Himself to do His work in us and through us. Let our chief work, as God's messengers, be intercession. In it we secure the presence and the power of God.

From *The Ministry of Intercession: A Plea for More Prayer*

13

Begin the Day with Prayer

By E. M. Bounds

He awakens Me morning by morning,
He awakens My ear to hear as the learned.
The Lord God has opened My ear.

ISAIAH 50:4–5 NKJV

The people who have done the most for God in this world have been early on their knees. He who fritters away the early morning in other pursuits than seeking God will make poor headway seeking Him throughout the rest of the day. If God is not first in our thoughts and efforts in the morning, He will be in last place for the remainder of the day.

Behind this early rising and early praying is the ardent desire which presses us into the pursuit of God. Morning listlessness is an indication of a listless heart. The heart which is hesitant to seek God in the morning has lost its relish for God.

David's heart was ardent for God. He hungered and thirsted after God, and so he sought God early, before daylight. The bed and sleep could not chain his soul in its eagerness to be with God.

Christ longed for communion with God; and so, rising a great while before day, He would go out to the mountain to pray. The disciples, when fully awake and ashamed of their indulgence, would know where to find Him. We might go through the list of men who have mightily impressed the world for God, and we would find them early seeking God.

A desire for God which cannot break the chains of sleep is a weak thing and will do little good for God after it has indulged itself fully. The person whose desire for God falls behind at the beginning of the day will never catch up.

From *Power Through Prayer*

14

The Secret of Prayer: A Knowledge of the Fatherhood of God

By Andrew Murray

Every good gift and every perfect gift is from above, and cometh down from the Father of lights.

James 1:17 KJV

Above all, let us hold fast to this blessed truth: that the knowledge of the Fatherhood of God —the revelation of His infinite Fatherliness in our hearts, the faith in the infinite love that gives us His Son and His Spirit to make us children—is indeed the secret of prayer. This is the new and living way

Christ opened up for us. To have Christ the Son—and the Spirit of the Son—dwelling within us, and revealing the Father, this makes us true, spiritual worshippers.

Blessed Jesus, I rejoice in the assurance that You will instruct Your disciple, who comes to You with a heart that longs to pray in spirit and in truth. O my Holy Master, teach me this blessed secret. Teach me that the worship in spirit and truth is not of man, but that it only comes from You. Teach me that prayer is not only a thing of times and seasons, but that it is the outflowing of a life in You.

Teach me to draw near to You, Jesus, in prayer under the deep impression of my ignorance. I am a child and have a child's liberty of access; in You I have the spirit of Sonship and of worship of truth. Teach me, above all, Blessed Son of the Father, how it is the revelation of the Father that gives confidence in prayer. And let the infinite Fatherliness of God's heart be my joy and my strength for a life of prayer and of worship.

From *The Ministry of Intercession: A Plea for More Prayer*

15

The Lord's Prayer: The Model Prayer to the Father

By Andrew Murray

After this manner therefore pray ye:
Our Father which art in heaven . . .

MATTHEW 6:9 KJV

Every teacher knows the power of example. The teacher not only tells the child what to do and how to do it, but also shows the student how it really can be done. In condescension to our weakness, our heavenly Teacher has given us the very words we are to take with us as we draw near to our Father.

We have in these words a form of prayer in which there breathe the freshness and fullness of the Eternal Life. It is a prayer so simple that the child can lisp it, so divinely rich that it comprehends all that God can give. It is a prayer that becomes the model and inspiration for all other prayers, and yet it always draws us back to itself as the deepest utterance of our souls before our God.

"Our Father which art in heaven!" To appreciate these words, I must remember that none of the saints in Scripture had ever ventured to address God as their Father. The invocation places us at once in the center of this wonderful revelation: the Son came to make His Father our Father too. These words are the key to the whole prayer, to all prayer. It takes time, it takes life to study them; it will take eternity to understand them fully.

The knowledge of God's Father-love is the first and simplest, but also the last and highest lesson in the school of prayer. It is in the personal relation to the living God, and in the personal conscious fellowship of love with Himself, that prayer begins. It is in the knowledge of God's Fatherliness, revealed by the Holy Spirit, that the power of prayer will be found to root and grow. In the infinite tenderness and pity and patience of the infinite Father, in His loving readiness to hear and to help, the life of prayer has its joy.

O let us take sufficient time, until the Spirit has made these words to fill our hearts: "Our Father which art in heaven." Then, we are indeed within the veil, in the secret place of power where prayer always prevails.

The Lord's Prayer

Our Father which art in heaven, Hallowed be thy name.

Thy kingdom come, Thy will be done in earth, as it is in heaven.

Give us this day our daily bread.

And forgive us our debts, as we forgive our debtors.

And lead us not into temptation, but deliver us from evil: For thine is the kingdom, and the power, and the glory, for ever. Amen.

MATTHEW 6:9–13 KJV

From *Lord, Teach Us to Pray*

16

God Will Not Cast Out Your Prayers

By John Wesley

If my people, which are called by my name, shall humble themselves, and pray, and seek my face, and turn from their wicked ways; then will I hear from heaven, and will forgive their sin, and will heal their land.

2 CHRONICLES 7:14 KJV

God will not cast out your prayers. No, perhaps He may say in the next hour, "Be of good cheer, thy sins are forgiven thee." Whatsoever your sins be, "though red like crimson" (Isaiah 1:18), though more than the hairs of your head, "return unto the

Lord, and he will have mercy upon [you], and to our God, for he will abundantly pardon" (Isaiah 55:7).

A Parable About Persistent Prayer

Then He spoke a parable to them, that men always ought to pray and not lose heart, saying: "There was in a certain city a judge who did not fear God nor regard man. Now there was a widow in that city; and she came to him, saying, 'Get justice for me from my adversary.' And he would not for a while; but afterward he said within himself, 'Though I do not fear God nor regard man, yet because this widow troubles me I will avenge her, lest by her continual coming she weary me.'"

Then the Lord said, "Hear what the unjust judge said. And shall God not avenge His own elect who cry out day and night to Him, though He bears long with them? I tell you that He will avenge them speedily.

LUKE 18:1–8 NKJV

You shall march on, under the great Captain of

your salvation, conquering and to conquer, until all your enemies are destroyed, and "death is swallowed up in victory" (1 Corinthians 15:54).

Now, thanks be to God, which gives us the victory through our Lord Jesus Christ; to whom, with the Father and the Holy Ghost, be blessing, and glory, and wisdom, and thanksgiving, and honor, and power, and might, forever and ever. Amen.

From *Salvation by Faith*

17

Prayer Marks Spiritual Leadership

By E. M. Bounds

I desire therefore that the men pray everywhere, lifting up holy hands, without wrath and doubting.

1 TIMOTHY 2:8 NKJV

The apostles knew the necessity and worth of prayer to their ministry. They knew that their high commission as apostles, instead of relieving them from the necessity of prayer, committed them to it by a more urgent need. They were exceedingly jealous else some other important work should exhaust their time and prevent their praying as they ought. So the apostles appointed laymen to look after the delicate and engrossing duties of ministering to the poor, so that they (the apostles) might, unhindered, "give [themselves] continually to prayer and to the ministry of the word" (Acts 6:4). Prayer was put first, and their relation to prayer was put most strongly, making a business of it, surrendering themselves to praying, putting fervor, urgency, perseverance, and time into it.

Apostolic people devoted themselves to the divine work of prayer. "Night and day praying exceedingly," says Paul (1 Thessalonians 3:10). How these New Testament preachers laid themselves out in prayer for God's people! How they put God in full force into their churches by their praying! These holy apostles did not vainly fancy that they had met their high and solemn duties by delivering faithfully God's word. Instead, their preaching was made to stick and tell by the ardor and insistence of their praying.

Apostolic praying was as taxing, toilsome, and imperative as apostolic preaching. The apostles prayed mightily day and night to bring their people to the highest regions of faith and holiness. They prayed mightier still to hold their people to this high spiritual altitude.

The preacher who has never learned in the school of Christ the high and divine art of intercession for his people will never learn the art of preaching, though homiletics be poured into him by the ton, and though he be the most gifted genius in sermon making and sermon delivery.

The prayers of apostolic, saintly leaders do much in making saints of those who are not apostles. Apostolic praying makes apostolic saints and keeps apostolic times of purity and power in the Church. What loftiness of soul, what purity and elevation of motive, what unselfishness, what self-sacrifice, what exhaustive toil, what ardor of spirit, what divine tact are all required to be an intercessor for people!

From *Prayer Through Power*

18

Learning to Pray Without Ceasing

By Andrew Murray

For God did not appoint us to wrath, but to obtain salvation through our Lord Jesus Christ, who died for us, that whether we wake or sleep, we should live together with Him. Therefore comfort each other and edify one another, just as you also are doing. And we urge you, brethren, to recognize those who labor among you, and are over you in the Lord and admonish you, and to esteem them very highly in love for their work's sake. Be at peace among yourselves.

Now we exhort you, brethren, warn those who are unruly, comfort the fainthearted, uphold the weak, be patient with all. See that no one renders evil for evil to anyone, but always pursue what is good both for yourselves and for all. Rejoice always, pray without ceasing, in everything give thanks; for this is the will of God in Christ Jesus for you. Do not quench the Spirit. Do not despise prophecies. Test all things; hold fast what is good. Abstain from every form of evil.

1 THESSALONIANS 5: 9-21 (NKJV)

Pray without ceasing. How can I learn it? The best way of learning to do a thing—in fact the only way—is to do it.

Begin by setting apart some time every day, say ten or fifteen minutes, in which you say to God and to yourself that you will come to Him as an intercessor for others. Let it be after your morning or evening prayer, or any other time.

If you cannot secure the same time every day, be not troubled. Only see that you do your work. Christ chose you and appointed you to pray for others.

If at first you do not feel any special urgency or faith or power in your prayers, do not let that hinder you. Quietly tell your Lord Jesus of your weakness; believe that the Holy Spirit is in you to teach you to pray; and, be assured that if you begin, God will help you.

From *The Ministry of Intercession: A Plea for More Prayer*

19

GOD WANTS THE WHOLE HEART

By Andrew Murray

For it is written, "You shall worship the LORD your God, and Him only you shall serve."

MATTHEW 4:10 NKJV

A Christian may often have very earnest desires for spiritual blessings. But alongside these are other desires in his daily life, desires that occupy a large place in his interests and affections. The spiritual desires are not all-absorbing. And, he wonders that his prayer is not heard. The answer, simply put, is that God wants the whole heart.

When the scribe asked Jesus to name the first commandment, our Master answered, "The first of all the commandments is: 'Hear, O Israel, the LORD our God, the LORD is one. And you shall love the LORD your God with all your heart, with all your soul, with all your mind, and with all your strength.' This is the first commandment" (Mark 12:29-30 NKJV). That law is unchangeable.

God offers Himself, gives Himself away, to the wholehearted who give themselves wholly away to Him. He always gives us according to our heart's desire, yet not as we think it, but as He sees it. If there are other desires that are more important to us, desires which have our hearts more than Himself, He allows those desires to be fulfilled, and the desires that engage us at the hour of prayer cannot be granted.

If we desire the gift of intercession and the power to pray aright, our hearts must be drawn away from other desires. We must give ourselves wholly to the Lord. We must be willing to live wholly in intercession for the kingdom. By fixing our eyes on the blessedness and the need of this grace, by thinking of the certainty that God will give it us, by giving ourselves up to it for the sake of the perishing world, then the first step is taken towards the possession of the coveted blessing.

Let us seek the grace of prayer, as we seek the God with whom it will link us, "with our whole desire." We may depend upon the promise, "He will fulfil the desire of them that fear Him." Let us never be afraid to say to Him, "I desire it with my whole heart."

From *The Ministry of Intercession: A Plea for More Prayer*

20

PRAY FOR HUMILITY

By John Wesley

The greatest among you must be a servant.
But those who exalt themselves will be humbled,
and those who humble themselves will be exalted.

MATTHEW 23:11–12 NKJV

Do not be afraid to know any evil that dwells in your own heart. Do not be afraid to know yourself as you are also known. Ask God for humility, so that you may not think of yourself more highly than you ought. Let your continual prayer be:

Show me, as my soul can bear,
The depth of inbred sin;
All the unbelief declare,
The pride that lurks within.

And when God hears your prayer and unveils your heart—when He shows you thoroughly what you are—then beware that your faith does not fail you. Hold your humility as a shield. Be abased. Be humbled in the dust. See yourself as nothing, as less than nothing. But still, "Let not your heart be troubled, neither let it be afraid" (John 14:27, KJV).

Hold fast and remember these words: "We have an Advocate with the Father, Jesus Christ the righteous" (1 John 2:1, NKJV).

And remember that, "As the heavens are higher than the earth" (Isaiah 55:9), so is His love higher than even my sins. Therefore, God is merciful to you a sinner. God is love; and Christ has died! Therefore, the Father Himself loves you!

From *The First Fruits of the Spirit*

21
Praying Is Spiritual Work

By E. M. Bounds

But thanks be to God, who gives us the victory through our Lord Jesus Christ.

Therefore, my beloved brethren, be steadfast, immovable, always abounding in the work of the Lord, knowing that your labor is not in vain in the Lord.

1 CORINTHIANS 15:57–58 NKJV

Praying is spiritual work. And human nature does not like taxing, spiritual work. Human nature wants to sail to heaven under a favoring breeze, on a full, smooth sea.

Prayer is humbling work. It abases intellect and pride, and it crucifies vanity. These are hard things for flesh and blood to bear. It is easier not to pray than to bear them. And so it is that we fall victim to one of the crying evils of these times, maybe of all times: little or no praying. Of these two evils, perhaps little praying is worse than no praying. Little praying is a kind of make-believe, a salve for the conscience, a farce and a delusion. The little value we put on prayer is evident from the little time we give to it.

The time given to prayer by the average servant scarcely counts in the sum of the daily aggregate. Not infrequently the servant's only praying is by his bedside in his nightdress, ready for bed and soon in it, with, perchance the addition of a few hasty snatches of prayer in the morning. How feeble, vain, and little is such praying compared with the time and energy devoted to prayer by holy men in and out of the Bible!

From *Power Through Prayer*

22

Thy Will Be Done

By Andrew Murray

After this manner therefore pray ye: Our Father which art in heaven, hallowed be thy name. Thy kingdom come, Thy will be done in earth, as it is in heaven.

MATTHEW 6:9-10 KJV

There is something here that strikes us at once. While we ordinarily first bring our own needs to God in prayer—and then we think of what belongs to God and His interests—the Master reverses the order. First, we are to pray *Thy* name, *Thy* kingdom, and *Thy* will. Then, and only then, are we to ask the Lord to give, to forgive, to lead, and to deliver. This lesson is of more importance than we think. In true worship, the Father must be first, must be all.

The sooner I learn to forget myself in the desire that He may be glorified, the richer will be the blessings that prayer will bring. No one ever loses by what he sacrifices for the Father. This fact must influence all our prayers.

There are two sorts of prayer: personal and intercessory. The latter ordinarily occupies the lesser part of our time and energy. This should not be. Christ has opened the school of prayer specially to train intercessors for the great work of bringing down—by their faith and prayers—the blessings of His work and love on the world around them. There can be no deep growth unless intercessory prayer becomes our primary focus.

The little child may ask of the father only what it needs for itself; and yet it soon learns to say, "Give some for sister, too." But the grown-up son, who only lives for the father's interest and takes charge of the father's business, asks more largely, and gets all that is asked.

Jesus would train us to the blessed life of consecration and service, in which our interests are all subordinate to the Name, and to the Kingdom, and to the Will of the Father. O let us live for this, and let us, with each act of adoration, follow in the same breath, "Thy Name, Thy Kingdom, Thy Will." It is for the will of the Father that we must look up and long.

From *Lord, Teach Us to Pray*

23

A Ministry of Prayer

By E. M. Bounds

Go therefore and make disciples of all the nations, baptizing them in the name of the Father and of the Son and of the Holy Spirit, teaching them to observe all things that I have commanded you; and lo, I am with you always, even to the end of the age.

MATTHEW 28:19–20 NKJV

The superficial results of many a ministry—and the deadness of others—are to be found in the lack of praying. No ministry can succeed without much praying, and this praying must be fundamental, ever abiding, ever increasing. The text, the sermon, should be the result of prayer. The study should be bathed in prayer, all its duties so impregnated with prayer, its whole spirit the spirit of prayer.

"I am sorry that I have prayed so little," was the deathbed regret of one of God's chosen ones, a sad and remorseful regret for a preacher. "I want a life of greater, deeper, truer prayer," said the late Archbishop Tait. So may we all say, and this may we all secure.

God's true preachers have been distinguished by one great feature: they were men of prayer. Differing often in many things, they have always had a common center. They may have started from different points, and traveled by different roads, but they converged to one point: they were one in prayer. God to them was the center of attraction, and prayer was the path that led to God. These men did not pray occasionally—nor did they pray a little at regular times or sporadically at odd times. They so prayed that their prayers entered into and shaped their characters; they so prayed as to affect their own lives and the lives of others; they so prayed as to make the history of the Church and to influence the current of the times.

God's true preachers spent much time in prayer, not because they marked the shadow on the dial or the hands on the clock, but because it was to them so momentous and engaging a business that they could scarcely resist it. Prayer was to them what it was to Paul, a striving with earnest effort of the soul. Prayer was to them what it was to Jacob, a wrestling and prevailing. Prayer was to them what it was to Christ: "with strong crying and tears" (Hebrews 5:7 KJV). God's true preachers prayed "always with all prayer and supplication in the Spirit, and watching thereunto with all perseverance" (Ephesians 6:18).

"The effectual fervent prayer" has been the mightiest weapon of God's mightiest soldiers. Let us consider the life of Elijah, who was "a man subject to like passions as we are, and he prayed earnestly that it might not rain: and it rained not on the earth by the space of three years and six months. And he prayed again, and the heaven gave rain, and the earth brought forth her fruit" (James 5:16–18 KJV).

Elijah exemplifies all the prophets and preachers who have moved their generation for God. May we be ever mindful of the instrument by which all these prophets worked their wonders.

From *Power Through Prayer*

24

Pray Sincerely and Privately

By John Wesley

And when you pray, you shall not be like the hypocrites. For they love to pray standing in the synagogues and on the corners of the streets, that they may be seen by men. Assuredly, I say to you, they have their reward. But you, when you pray, go into your room, and when you have shut your door, pray to your Father who is in the secret place; and your Father who sees in secret will reward you openly.

MATTHEW 6:5–6 (NKJV)

Hypocrisy and insincerity are the first things we are to guard against in prayer. Beware not to speak what you do not mean. Prayer is the lifting up of the heart to God. All words of prayer, without this lifting up of the heart, are mere hypocrisy. Whenever, therefore, you attempt to pray, see that your one design is to commune with God, to lift up your heart to him, to pour out your soul before him.

Do not imitate the hypocrites, who love, or are wont, "to pray standing in the synagogues," or in the exchange, or in the market-places, or "on the corners of the streets." They pray wherever the most people are, "that they may be seen by men." This was the sole design, the motive, and end, of the prayers which those hypocrites repeated.

"Verily I say unto you," says Jesus, "they have their reward" (Matthew 6:5 KJV). And since the hypocrites have already received their earthly reward, they are to expect none from the Father which is in heaven.

Perhaps no sin of omission is more common than the neglect of private prayer; the lack of which cannot be supplied in any other way. Our spiritual growth does not continue, much less increase, unless we use all opportunities of communing with Him, and pouring out our hearts before Him.

If, therefore, we neglect private prayer—if

we allow business, company, or any avocation whatsoever to prevent these secret exercises of the soul—then life will surely decay.

From *Upon Our Lord's Sermon on the Mount*
and from *The Wilderness State*

25

God's Presence in Prayer

By Andrew Murray

I am not alone, because the Father is with me.

JOHN 16:32 KJV

God is a God who hides Himself from the carnal eye. So when we worship Him, if we are chiefly occupied with our own thoughts and exercises, we shall not meet Him who is a Spirit, the unseen One. But to the man who withdraws himself from all that is of the world and man, and who prepares to wait upon God alone, the Father will reveal Himself.

If a man shuts out the world, and the life of the

world, and surrenders himself to be led by Christ into the secret of God's presence, the light of the Father's love will rise upon him. The secrecy of the inner chamber and the closed door—the entire separation from all around us—is an image of that inner spiritual sanctuary where our spirit truly comes into contact with the Invisible One. And so we are taught, at the very outset of our search after the secret of effectual prayer, to remember that it is in the inner chamber, where we are alone with the Father, that we shall learn to pray aright. The Father is in secret: in these words Jesus teaches us where He is waiting for us, where He is always to be found.

Christians often complain that their private prayer is not what it should be. They feel weak and ineffectual; the heart is cold and dark; it is as if they have so little to pray, and in those prayers no faith or joy. They are discouraged and kept from prayer by the thought that they cannot come to the Father as they ought or as they wish.

Child of God, listen to your Teacher. He tells you that when you go to private prayer your first thought must be the Father. If your heart is cold, get into the presence of the loving Father. As a father pities his children, so the Lord pities you. Do not be thinking of how little you have to bring God, but think, instead, about how much He wants to give you. Just place yourself before Him and look up into His face; think of His love, His wonderful, tender, pitying love. It is the Father's loving heart that will give light and warmth to yours. Just do what Jesus says: Just shut the door and pray to thy Father, which is in secret. Is it not wonderful? Yes, it is wonderful to be alone with God, your infinite, loving Father.

From *Lord, Teach Us to Pray*

26

PRAYER: THE MOST IMPORTANT THING WE CAN DO

By E. M. Bounds

For the eyes of the LORD are on the righteous,
and His ears are open to their prayers.

1 PETER 3:12 NKJV

More time and early hours for prayer would act like magic to revive and invigorate many a decayed spiritual life. More time and early hours for prayer would be manifest in holy living. A holy life would not be so rare or so difficult a thing if our devotions were not so short and hurried. A Christ-like temper would not be so rare if our closeted prayers were lengthened and intensified. We live shabbily because we pray sparingly.

Time spent feasting in our closets will bring health to our lives. Our ability to stay with God in our closet measures our ability to stay with Him throughout the rest of the day. Hasty closet visits are deceptive and defaulting. We are not only deluded by them, but we are losers by them in many ways and in many rich legacies. Tarrying in the closet instructs and wins. We are taught by it, and the greatest victories are often the results of great waiting—waiting till words and plans are exhausted. Silent and patient waiting gains the crown. Jesus Christ asks with an affronted emphasis, "Shall not God avenge his own elect which cry day and night unto him" (Luke 18:7 KJV)?

To pray is the greatest thing we can do. And to do it well there must be calmness, time, and deliberation; otherwise it is degraded into the littlest and meanest of things. True praying has the largest results for good, and poor praying the least.

We cannot do too much of real praying; we cannot do too little of the sham. We must learn anew the worth of prayer, enter anew the school of prayer. There is nothing which takes more time to learn. And if we are to learn the wondrous art, we must not give a fragment here and there. Instead, we must grasp the best hours of the day for God and prayer, or there will be no praying worth the name.

From *Power Through Prayer*

27

THE POWER OF PRAYER COMES FROM GOD

By John Wesley

Therefore humble yourselves under the mighty hand of God, that He may exalt you in due time, casting all your care upon Him, for He cares for you.

1 PETER 5:6-7 NKJV

It is God alone who, by His own almighty power, works in us to achieve what is pleasing in His sight. And all outward thing—unless the Lord works in them and by them—are weak and beggarly elements. If we imagine, therefore, that there is any intrinsic power in any means other than the Lord, we are mistaken, and we lack a knowledge of God's power.

We know that there is no inherent power in the words that are spoken in prayer, in the letter of Scripture read, in the sound of Scripture heard, or in the bread and wine received in the Lord's Supper. But it is God alone who is the Giver of every good gift and the Author of all grace. If there is any blessing conveyed to our soul, the whole power is of Him.

All who desire the grace of God are to wait for it in the way of prayer. This is the express direction of our Lord himself. In His Sermon upon the Mount, after explaining at large wherein religion consists, and describing the main branches of it, He adds, "Ask, and it shall be given you; seek, and ye shall find; knock, and it shall be opened unto you: For everyone that asketh receiveth; and he that seeketh findeth; and to him that knocketh it shall be opened" (Matthew 7:7–8 KJV).

Here we are in the plainest manner directed to ask, in order to—or as a means of—receiving. We are instructed *to seek* in order *to find* the grace of God, the pearl of great price. We are directed to knock, to continue asking and seeking, if we wish to enter into His kingdom.

From *The Means of Grace*

28

The Life That Can Pray

By Andrew Murray

You will show me the path of life;
in Your presence is fullness of joy;
at Your right hand are pleasures forevermore.

PSALM 16:11 NKJV

Just think for a moment of the men of prayer in Scripture, and see in them—and see what their lives were—that they could pray with such power. We spoke of Abraham as intercessor. What gave Him such boldness? He knew that God had chosen and called him away from his home and people to walk before Him, that all nations might be blessed in him. He knew that he had obeyed, and forsaken all for God. Implicit obedience, to the very sacrifice of his son, was the law of his life. He did what God asked: he dared trust God to do what he asked.

We spoke of Moses as intercessor. He too had forsaken all for God. He lived at God's disposal: "as a servant he was faithful in all His house." It is written of Moses, "According to all the Lord commanded him, so did he" (Exodus 40:16). No wonder Moses was very bold: his heart was right with God, and he knew God would hear him. This also holds true for Elijah, the man who stood up to plead for the Lord God of Israel. Elijah was ready to risk all for God, and he counted upon God to do all for him.

It is as men live that they pray. It is the life that prays. It is the life that, with whole hearted devotion, gives up all for God and to God. It is this kind of life that can claim all from God.

Our God longs exceedingly to prove Himself the Faithful God and Mighty Helper of His people. He only waits for hearts that are wholly turned from the world to Himself, and thus open to receive His gifts. The man who loses all will find all. The branch that only and truly lives abiding in Christ, the Heavenly Vine—entirely given up, like Christ, to bear fruit in the salvation of men—may ask what it will, and it shall be done.

And even though we have not yet attained that full devotion to which our Lord had trained His disciples, and therefore cannot equal them in their power of prayer, we may, nevertheless, take courage in remembering that every new onward step in the striving after the perfect branch-life will be met from above by a corresponding liberty to draw greater boldness, and to expect larger answers. The more we pray, and the more conscious we become of our unfitness to pray in power, the more we shall be urged and helped to press on towards the secret of power in prayer—a life abiding in Christ entirely at His disposal.

From *The Ministry of Intercession: A Plea for More Prayer*

29

The Need for Praying Christians

By E. M. Bounds

Watch ye therefore, and pray always.

LUKE 21:36 KJV

Never has the need been greater for saintly men and women. More imperative still is the call for saintly, God-devoted preachers. The world moves with gigantic strides. Satan has his hold and rule on the world, and labors to make all its movements serve his ends. So religion must do its best work while presenting its most attractive and perfect models. By every means, modern sainthood must be inspired by the loftiest ideals and by the largest possibilities through the Spirit.

Paul lived on his knees so that the Ephesian Church might measure the heights, breadths, and depths of an unmeasurable saintliness, and "be filled with all the fullness of God" (Ephesians 3:19 NKJV)

Epaphras laid himself out with the exhaustive toil and strenuous conflict of fervent prayer so that the Colossian Church might "stand perfect and complete in all the will of God" (Colossians 4:12).

Everywhere, everything in apostolic times was focused on prayer so that the people of God might each and "all come in the unity of the faith, and of the knowledge of the Son of God, unto a perfect man, unto the measure of the stature of the fullness of Christ" (Ephesians 4:13 KJV). No premium was given to small efforts; no encouragement to immaturity. The children were to grow; the old, instead of feebleness and infirmities, were to bear fruit in old age. The need for holy men and holy women was great.

No amount of money, genius, or culture can move things for God. Holiness energizing the soul, energizing the whole man aflame with love, with desire for more faith, more prayer, more zeal, and more consecration—this is the secret of power. These we need and must have. And men must be the incarnation of this God-inflamed devotedness.

From *Power Through Prayer*